D1685687

IFLL
Inquiry into the Future
for Lifelong Learning

Crime and Lifelong Learning

IFLL Thematic Paper 5

Professor Tom Schuller

© 2009 National Institute of Adult Continuing Education

(England and Wales)

21 De Montfort Street

Leicester

LE1 7GE

Company registration no. 2603322

Charity registration no. 1002775

NIACE has a broad remit to promote lifelong learning opportunities for adults. NIACE works to develop increased participation in education and training, particularly for those who do not have easy access because of class, gender, age, race, language and culture, learning difficulties or disabilities, or insufficient financial resources.

You can find NIACE online at www.niace.org.uk

Cataloguing in Publication Data

A CIP record of this title is available from the British Library

Designed and typeset by Creative by Design, Paisley, Scotland

Printed and bound in the UK

ISBN: 978 1 86201 415 2

Contents

Foreword

This is the fifth Thematic Paper to be published from the Inquiry into the Future for Lifelong Learning (IFLL). The Inquiry was established in September 2007 and will make its main report in September 2009. It is sponsored by NIACE, the National Institute of Adult Continuing Education, with an independent Board of Commissioners under the chairmanship of Sir David Watson. Full details of the IFLL can be found at: www.niace.org.uk/lifelonglearninginquiry.

The overall goal of the Inquiry is to offer **an authoritative and coherent strategic framework for lifelong learning in the UK**. This involves:

- articulating a broad rationale for public and private investment in lifelong learning;

- a re-appraisal of the social and cultural value attached to it by policy-makers and the public;

- developing new perspectives on policy and practice.

IFLL: supplementary papers

The Thematic Papers are complemented by several other strands of IFLL work:

- *Context Papers.* These will provide a broad overall picture of expenditure on all forms of lifelong learning: by government, across all departments; by employers, public and private; by the third sector; and by individuals and households. We shall provide, as a complement, a summary of overall participation. The two in combination should provide a benchmark for mapping future trends.

- *Sector Papers.* These discuss the implications of lifelong learning for each of the sectors involved in providing learning opportunities: pre-school, school, FE, HE, private trainers, and local authorities. The goal here is to encourage innovation thinking on how these parts do or do not fit together, as part of a systemic approach to lifelong learning.

- *Public Value Papers.* These will look, from different angles and using a variety of techniques, at the 'social productivity' of lifelong learning; i.e. what effects it has on areas such as health, civic activity or crime. The goal is both to provide evidence on these effects, and to stimulate a broader debate on how such effects can be measured and analysed.

- *Learning Infrastructures.* Unlike the others this strand consists not of a series of papers but of a set of scenarios, designed to promote debate and imagination on what the infrastructure for learning might look like in the future. This challenges us to integrate the physical environments of learning, the virtual environments of learning technologies, and people's competences and behaviour.

We have also been consulting in the four UK nations, and amongst learner groups and other stakeholders.

Published papers are available from the IFLL website:
www.lifelonglearninginquiry.org.uk

Thematic Papers

The Thematic Papers form the core initial substance of the Inquiry's work. They cover the following:

Prosperity, Employment and Work

Demography and Social Structure

Well-being and Happiness

Migration and Communities

Technological Change

Poverty Reduction

Citizenship and Belonging

Crime and Social Exclusion

Sustainable Development

Each of these themes has been tackled in the same way (except for the last, which will be treated separately): a call for evidence was issued; a day-long seminar was organised, with inputs from practitioners, policy-makers and researchers; and the results of these two stages, and subsequent discussions and contributions, are distilled into a Thematic Paper, written either by an IFLL Commissioner or a member of the IFLL Secretariat.

We have posted on the IFLL website the evidence submitted specifically to the Inquiry, along with the papers and presentations contributed to the thematic seminar.

Next steps

This Thematic Paper represents the culmination of one stage in the Inquiry's work on this strand. We are very grateful to all those who responded to the call for evidence, and who contributed subsequently to the seminar. However, we are very well aware that the process of debate and consultation has been limited. Some people will not have been aware of the call for evidence, or not had time to make a submission. Others will have waited until there were some conclusions to respond to. Therefore, the publication of this Thematic Paper is also an invitation for a second round of comment, submission and debate. Are there important issues which are not covered here? What further evidence should be included?

Conclusions from this paper will be incorporated into the Inquiry's main report, to be published in September 2009. Please join the debate on this theme and the Inquiry as a whole by sending your comments to lifelonglearninginquiry@niace.org.uk

Professor Tom Schuller
Director, IFLL

Sir David Watson
Chair, IFLL Commissioners

Executive summary

Crime and punishment cost us all a huge amount, economically, socially and personally. Prison populations have soared, taking us down a road from which it is difficult to retreat. Prisons are full of offenders with very low educational levels. Investing in better education and training opportunities gives hope, and makes good economic as well as social sense. However, despite some advances, this positive investment is currently not adequate, in quality or size.

Prevention and integration

Punishment is one function of penal policy. Learning relates to another: rehabilitation and reintegration. There is necessarily some tension between the two, especially if offenders are seen to be in some sense advantaged by being given access to learning; but this cannot be a reason for wasting such huge resources on non-productive incarceration.

Both general education and training and specific preventive interventions reduce the risks of people engaging in criminal activity and re-offending. The evidence on the level of effectiveness is varied: some derives from robust technical research, but there is also a mass of significant experience which should not be neglected.

Learning geared solely to change in individual offender behaviour and attitudes is only part of the story. We are all implicated, some directly as victims, family or community members, many more as citizens involved or compliant in shaping penal policy and debate. Lifelong learning's role should be seen in this broader context, of enabling informed public debate and decision.

Making lifelong learning an effective instrument against crime requires action on several fronts. Increasing human capital through skills and qualifications must go with improved social capital, building useful networks and peer/family support; and with building appropriate self-esteem and the belief in a better life ahead.

Learning will only have significant effect if linked with other policies, particularly on employment and accommodation. This is crucial at key transition points, particularly at the point of release. There is a strong case for all prisoners to be given access to education or training as a matter of course immediately when they leave prison, combined with pre-release preparation for it.

Offender learning

Learning provision should be needs-based, drawing on a wide range of teaching and delivery modes, to reflect the particular and diverse needs of offenders. There should be better diagnostic services, especially on an offender's first imprisonment, to identify learning difficulties.

Continuity, stability and progression are essential. Too many offenders have their studies interrupted, or find that they cannot move on to a further stage. Offenders on defined courses should not be moved during the course. A flexible credit-based system would help all of these goals.

Distance learning, for obvious reasons, has a major role to play. This also means encouraging innovation in the use of information and communication technologies (ICT). On this, and in many other respects, there are diverse voluntary sector initiatives which deserve strong support.

Mental health and well-being is a major issue for offenders, reflecting the multiple problems many of them bring, notably linked to alcohol and drug abuse. Developing health capabilities is a significant learning challenge for the population as a whole. It has particular implications for the offender population.

Personal development is a central goal not a frill, in addition to certificated and embedded skills training. Many initiatives show the results of approaches which allow offenders to explore their creativity.

For young people in particular, going into custody removes from them any public identity. Learning can help give offenders a positive identity, and stake in society. Developing learner accounts for offenders whilst they are in prison is a promising route to address this issue.

Prison staff, and other related professionals such as probation officers, themselves need training and education, at all levels including leadership. The workforce modernisation programme will be crucial. Staff should be seen as key intermediaries for lifelong learning, with a powerful role to play in encouraging and enabling offender education.

The experience of prisoners and ex-prisoners should be used for teaching and mentoring, inside and outside prison.

Finally, we need better and more analysis of the costs and benefits of offender learning, and of lifelong learning generally, in relation to crime and imprisonment. This should include more research which draws on multiple methods, and more public discussion of the estimates of costs and benefits.

1. Introduction[1]

The rationale for tackling the theme of crime is both very straightforward and extremely complex. It is straightforward in the sense that crime costs us all enormously, in many different ways: physically, psychologically, socially, financially and politically. It hits the victims, their families, friends and neighbourhoods. It damages the offenders, and their families, friends and neighbourhoods. And it punishes all of us, through the costs it imposes and the damage it inflicts on the social fabric. In this paper, we include some of the research which demonstrates the financial side of these costs; but these calculable costs are greatly surpassed by the personal and social wounds inflicted, which are far more difficult to assess in any quantifiable form. So anything that lifelong learning can do to reduce crime is almost certainly positive – only 'almost' because it is quite possible to envisage lifelong learning which achieves the crime reduction goal but at unacceptable cost to personal liberties.

The IFLL theme is titled 'crime and social exclusion'. In fact, this Thematic Paper concentrates on crime as an acute form of social exclusion, and has nothing to say directly about other forms of social exclusion.[2] This is primarily for reasons of space and time. But the key rationale is common across most forms of social exclusion: whilst there will always be disagreement over the precise reasons and moral responsibilities, there is no doubt that the costs of social exclusions are high; that they affect us all, however indirectly; that prevention and timely intervention are better than cure; and that learning brings hope.[3]

We should reject single-factor solutions. Most criminal activity is the product of multiple causes. These are deep-rooted, both in the sense that they are hard to eradicate and because they often stretch back a long way in the individual's life history. They also have deep social origins. We cannot here discuss the issue of responsibility for criminal behaviour, except to say that in almost every case it is a mix of personal responsibility and social conditions, and the mix will vary hugely – it is almost never purely one or the other. Lifelong learning's contribution to preventing crime and reducing recidivism covers a wide range: from programmes expressly designed to help specific offenders, to the overall distribution of educational opportunity. Making

---

[1] Special thanks for helpful comments to: Pat Jones (Prisoners' Education Trust), David Wilson (University of Birmingham), Andy Healey, Nalini Sharma and colleagues (Ministry of Justice), John Bynner (Longview), Chris Bath (Unlock), Phil Bayliss (University of Plymouth), Patsy Quinn (NIACE), Susan Quinn (NIACE), Mike Adler (University of Edinburgh), Kate Gavron.

[2] See Bynner (2009).

[3] Offenders are identified as a specific group in the PSA discussion of social exclusion. The reference to learning within this runs as follows: "The *Reducing Re-offending through Skills and Employment Next Steps Action Plan*, led jointly by DWP, DIUS and NOMS, focuses on improving offenders' employability, linking training to labour market needs, and providing offenders with a direct route into employment. Key priorities for delivery are to engage employers through the Reducing Re-offending Corporate Alliance, build on the new offender learning and skills service, and reinforce the emphasis on skills and jobs in prisons and probation." (PSA Delivery Agreement 16, 3.37, see http://www.cabinetoffice. gov.uk/media/cabinetoffice/social_exclusion_task_force/assets/chronic_exclusion/psa_da_16.pdf).

IFLL
Inquiry into the Future
for Lifelong Learning

sure that all have adequate chances at every stage is an obvious general goal. But we should not fall into the trap of thinking that because learning may be an important part of successful penal policy, it is all therefore a matter of enabling individuals to behave differently.

Penal policy has several functions: security for society, punishment and rehabilitation of offenders. The focus here is on the rehabilitation function, to which lifelong learning is most obviously relevant. However, there is a key further aspect. As with some of the other Inquiry themes (for example, migration, see McNair, 2009b), better learning for all should help a more informed debate on how a civilised society should behave – in this case, how it should treat its offenders.

1.1 The prison population

Sadly, there is a specific UK weight to the crime theme. Our prison population is abnormal by almost any standards – 'hyper-incarceration' is an apt term. Devolution has allowed some divergence, however, and Scotland's Criminal Justice System seems to be taking a somewhat different direction from that of England and Wales, with a clear intention of reducing prison numbers from its current, very high, level.[4] The prison population in January 2009 was 81,751 in England and Wales. It has grown by some 25 per cent in the last ten years. Around 245,000 other offenders were under supervision by the Probation Service.

Within that overall population, certain groups figure particularly prominently. Members of black and minority ethnic groups, notably, are hugely 'overrepresented' in prison. Women are 'underrepresented', but hardly in a way that we would wish to see corrected; their imprisonment rates are rising sharply. These overall trends (given in more detail in the following section) mean that more and more children (around 150,000) have parents in prison, which is hardly the best start in life for them and raises the likelihood of a cycle repeating itself. The figures mark us out from almost all other European countries, whose custody levels are proportionately far lower.

1.2 The role of education

Education does help to prevent criminal behaviour in the first place, or at least the criminal behaviour most commonly sanctioned by custodial sentence. This is because it helps to give people the capacity to earn a proper living; and because, at least to some extent, it reinforces norms which inhibit criminal behaviour.[5] Improving educational opportunities for all should prevent people engaging in crime in the first

---

[4] See *Scotland's Choice*, http://www.scotland.gov.uk/Publications/2008/06/30162955/2
[5] As noted in the introduction, the evidence on this is varied, notably on how far precise causality can be established. See Feinstein (2002) for an area-based econometric analysis of the impact of raising educational levels on crime, via wage effects. See also Machin, S. and Meghir, C. (2000), and for more general education-crime effects in the US, Lochner, L. and Moretti, E. (2001).

place and exercise downward pressure on offending levels. This is especially the case if we can improve learning opportunities for those most disadvantaged, who have the least evident stake in the system, as young people and as adults. But we should note, in all seriousness, that learning sometimes actually fosters crime. It provides the skills both to commit crimes, and to get away with them. As so-called 'white-collar' crime grows, so the direct as opposed to the inverse relationship between education and crime will grow.[6] This also points to the highly contentious issue of how crime is defined, and how far our punishment regime fits the crimes we know to be committed, but which go largely undetected and unpunished.

Recidivism rates are very high. Recidivism is by definition a mark of failure of rehabilitation, collective as well as individual, though of course it cannot be eliminated. A key part of the rationale is that education should help to reduce recidivism, whether through specific training programmes, through enhancing general skills and qualifications or because of a general effect of participation in learning on offenders' sense of respect for themselves and for others.

Our interest in the part that lifelong learning does or could play in relation to crime is not restricted to prevention or reduction of individual offending behaviour. It also concerns the part learning can play in helping all those with a stake in the system. One example is restorative justice, which helps offenders to make good to victims and to their communities, but also helps these to come to terms with the offender and his or her behaviour.[7] But there is a broader dimension: lifelong learning helps communities generally develop their capacity to think and debate issues surrounding crime in a more reasonable way. Learning does not inoculate against perversely punitive or absurdly permissive stances. It may not generate any greater degree of consensus on what is a very contentious set of issues, but it should help more civilised and informed debate, public and private, about what is right and wrong in relation to crime.

Wider reasoned debate is definitely needed. In his report on prison places, Lord Carter called for more public debate on the trade-offs involved:

> "The public and government are thus faced with the choice as to whether to increase continually the sums of public expenditure devoted to imprisonment or better to plan for, manage and use custody in a way that not only ensures the protection of the public and the punishment of offenders, but also the reduction of re-offending."[8]

And in a recent Prison Reform Trust lecture, Bryan Stevenson urged the UK not to let the current trend towards hyper-incarceration go undiscussed.[9] Formal and informal

---

[6] See, for example, Karstedt and Farrall (2007).
[7] For this as part of government policy on citizen empowerment, see http://www.hmg.gov.uk/media/15556/workingtogether.pdf, and http://www.cabinetoffice.gov.uk/media/cabinetoffice/strategy/assets/publications/world_class_public_services.pdf
[8] Carter (2007).
[9] Stevenson, B. From a lecture entitled *Warning from America: the social and economic impact of over-incarceration and how to avoid it,* Prison Reform Trust, see http://www.prisonreformtrust.org.uk/subsection.asp?id=1604

learning play a crucial part in promoting reasoned debate. It is, for example, a sign of hope when civic organisations such as the Women's Institute make it a priority theme. It is not too naïve to assert that education reduces damaging populism, and pushes up the standard of debate and decision-making. It should help in 'the fight to put ladders in place of walls at the edge of our society', as the Progress Policy Group defines the goal of penal policy.[10]

Therefore, the rationale is a mixture of the economic, the social and the moral. We cannot *afford* to allow the current trends to continue; we cannot *sustain* the level of damage done to the fabric of society; and we cannot *condone* the loss which crime inflicts on all concerned.

Lifelong learning has a part to play along all three dimensions. It should be able to reduce the economic costs; it should be able to help maintain the social fabric; and it should be able to maintain ethical and political (in the broad sense) debate at a level where we can make good decisions, individually and collectively. But – and this is a key theme throughout the Inquiry – it can have only limited impact on any of these on its own. So we need constant reminders that the quality and effectiveness of lifelong learning depends crucially on how far it can mesh in with other strands of policy and practice.

1.3 The effects of learning: raising human, social and identity capital

Evidence on how far lifelong learning does or could contribute to lower offending behaviour is highly variable. The mechanisms through which learning impacts on social outcomes such as crime are complex. The effect, such as it is, may come through indirect channels; for example, by increasing earnings potential and therefore enabling people to move to an environment where offending behaviour is less prevalent. More direct possible effects include giving the sense of a greater stake in society, greater self-efficacy and a stronger identification with social norms. It is extremely difficult to establish with certainty which of these mechanisms apply, and to what extent.[11]

One way of encompassing these effects is to bring into play the trio of capitals which is used elsewhere in Inquiry papers and in the wider debate on the benefits of learning.[12] Human capital is the economic asset of personal skills and qualifications, supplied mostly through individual education and training. Social capital is the set of networks and shared norms, often enhanced and expanded by participation in education. Identity capital is the sense of personal worth and belonging. Shortages of all of these forms of capital combine to reduce the chances of successful desistance.

[10] Progress Policy Group (2008).
[11] See OECD (2007a) on understanding the social outcomes of learning generally.
[12] See Schuller et al (2004) and the Inquiry's main report: Learning Through Life: The Inquiry into the Future for Lifelong Learning (Schuller and Watson, 2009).

Offenders have lower human capital. They tend to lack the qualifications to enable them to gain lawful employment, and the skills necessary to work productively. This effectively excludes them from the regular labour market, and from the prospect of progress in a conventional job. Two-thirds of prisoners leave prison with no job or training to go to. Similarly with social capital: it is lacking, or of a kind which promotes rather than discourages crime. Offenders' networks are often restricted to their offending peers, reinforcing rather than countering their previous outlook and behaviour. Forty-five per cent of those going through prison lose their marriage or relationship. Two-thirds of those who have a job lose it whilst in custody. They are cut off from, or rejected by, family and friends who might integrate them into society, and from the networks which would bring them job opportunities. The loss of these relationships reduces the odds of successful desistance enormously. Thirdly, their sense of self-worth is often either poor or misguided, so their identity capital is low. The combination of low capital of all three kinds is, to use a currently prominent term, toxic.

IFLL
Inquiry into the Future
for Lifelong Learning

2. Current situation

2.1 The prison population

This Thematic Paper cannot deal with penal policy overall; but from the point of view of offender learning, there can be no doubt that the sheer size of the prison population is a huge barrier to effective practice. Many prisoners should be dealt with elsewhere, notably those with mental health and addiction problems.[13] The inclusion in the prison population of large numbers of such people means that neither they nor other offenders can be given effective learning opportunities. One particularly significant aspect of this is that prison staff have demands made on them which they are simply not qualified to meet.

Figure 1: Annual average prison population (1901–2005)[14]

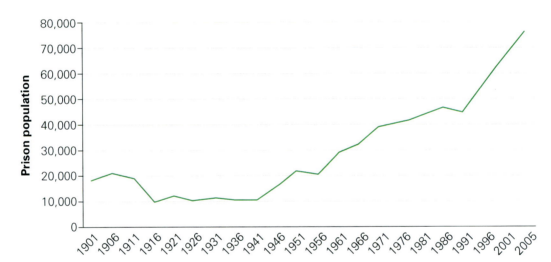

The general trend is very well known, and just as disturbing. Within this overall rise, the position in relation to some sub-groups needs brief elaboration.

Young people

Every year, 70,000 people of school age enter the youth justice system. The age of criminal responsibility is 12 in England and as low as ten in Scotland. In most European countries it is substantially higher. The average population of children in penal custody in England and Wales is around 3,000.[15] In September 2008 there were 2,399 15–17 year olds in prison. Most of these have a background of multiple social exclusion,

---

[13] Sainsbury Centre (2009a).
[14] Source: Home Office: http://rds.homeoffice.gov.uk/rds/pdfs/psewtabs.pdf
[15] Howard League for Penal Reform (2007).

including domestic violence. This generates enormous pressures on containment: the Youth Justice Board spends over ten times more on custody than on crime prevention programmes.

Ethnicity

Members of black and minority ethnic groups are heavily overrepresented in custody, especially in certain areas. They are also more likely to be victims of crime. African-Caribbean youth are greatly overrepresented both amongst victims and offenders in violent crime against young people.[16] Fifteen per cent of male and 21 per cent of female prisoners are black or black British, and a further seven per cent and two per cent Asian/British-Asian.

A far higher percentage of black inmates (28 per cent in 2005) than white (13 per cent) are on drug offence charges, though the black community has a per capita drug use below that of whites.

In 2002, black and minority ethnic women made up eight per cent of the UK population, but 31 per cent of the female prison population.

Gender

The number of women in prison has doubled over the last ten years, to just under 5,000[17]. More than half of women in UK prisons say that they have suffered domestic violence and one in three has experienced sexual abuse. Two out of three women in prison have dependent children. Just five per cent of women prisoners' children remain in their own home once their mother has been sentenced. There are no women's prisons in Wales, so that family rupture is even more prevalent for Welsh families.

The educational achievement of women prisoners is lower than for male prisoners. Seventy-four per cent left school at 16 or before. Only 39 per cent have any qualifications at all, compared to 82 per cent of the general population. Forty-one per cent of women prisoners have not worked in the past five years.

Age

The fastest growing age group in prison are those aged over 50. Whilst remarkable, this is not often remarked upon: *'No problems – old and quiet'* was the title of a 2004 report from HMIP on older prisoners[18]. The rise is because sentences are becoming longer, and sometime indeterminate, in addition to the general growth trend. In 2008

---

[16] See Mayor of London (2008) *Time for Action*; http://www.london.gov.uk/mayor/crime/timeforaction/docs/timeforaction-main.pdf
[17] Howard League for Penal Reform (2006).
[18] HM Inspectorate of Prisons (2004); see also Prison Reform Trust (2008).

there were 6661 men and 316 women aged over 50 in prison in England and Wales; the numbers of men over 60 has tripled since 1996. Most of them suffer from a mental health condition.

Mental health

The levels of mental ill-health in the prison population are exceptionally high. Depending on what measures are used, it is estimated that around 70 per cent of prisoners have a mental health problem[19]. At any one time, around ten per cent of the prison population have serious mental health problems.

Table 1: Prevalence of mental health problems[20]

Prevalence among prisoners		Prevalence in general population (adults of working age)
Schizophrenia and delusional disorder	8%	0.5%
Personality disorder	66%	5.3%
Neurotic disorder (e.g. depression)	45%	13.8%
Drug dependency	45%	5.2%
Alcohol dependency	30%	11.5%

In 2007, ten per cent of men and 30 per cent of women have had previous psychiatric admission before they came into prison. The level of psychotic disorder is between 14 and 23 times that of the general population.

Substance abuse

The prevalence of alcohol and drug abuse/dependence in male and female prisoners is far higher than in the general population. Separate but heavily overlapping with the previous section are those involved in drug and alcohol abuse. High proportions of prisoners are convicted of drug offences (26 per cent of all female prisoners), whilst many other offences are linked directly to drugs or alcohol. In nearly half of violent crimes reported to the 2004/5 British Crime Survey, the victim believed the attacker to be under the influence of alcohol (18 per cent for drugs). Drinking is involved in many crimes, especially violent ones that lead to prison. Thirty-four per cent of prisoners in Scotland have indicated their drinking was a problem outside, and 44 per cent that they were drunk at the time of offence.[21] Forty per cent of female remand prisoners report having injected drugs, 34 per cent regularly.

---

[19] Prison Reform Trust (2009).
[20] Source: Singleton et al. (1998); cited in Sainsbury Centre (2008a).
[21] Prison Reform Trust, *Bromley Briefings*, December 2008.

Finally, many of these characteristics of course overlap, representing multiple problems. For example, young offenders have high levels of mental health problems, which often call for family intervention strategies. The demands on prisons rise steeply in the face of such multiple difficulties.

2.2 A successful investment?

What are the costs? The total prisons expenditure has risen from £2.843 billion in 1995 to £4.325 billion in 2006 (2006 prices). The direct cost of keeping someone in prison is usually estimated at between £35,000 and £40,000 per year. This excludes costs of the crime to victims, of supporting families whilst the offender is in custody, and of unemployment, substance abuse and homelessness. In its submission to the IFLL, Southampton City Council estimates total costs conservatively at £100,000 per offender.[22] The 2002 Social Exclusion Unit (SEU) estimate was £90,000 per young offender in custody.[23] As for the long term, keeping someone in prison for 30 years costs an estimated £1 million. Even in today's volatile economic times, these do not look like a good investment. Broader cost-benefit analyses would throw up far greater figures still.

The costs are huge. Does it work? There is no simple way of judging this. The numbers who continue to offend are relevant – bearing in mind that rehabilitation to reduce reoffending is only one of the objectives of imprisonment – but they are not always easily calculated. Reconviction rates are a crude measure, but they are very high.

The SEU report, *Reducing Re-Offending by Prisoners,* found that recorded crime alone committed by ex-prisoners came to £11 billion annually. In Scotland in 2002–3 23 per cent of the 45,000 offenders discharged from custody or given non-custodial sentences were reconvicted within six months, and 45 per cent within two years.[24] In 2006–07, nearly 7,000 offenders who received a custodial sentence had already accumulated between them 47,500 prior spells in prison! The England and Wales figures are higher – 58.5 per cent are reconvicted within two years. Sixty-eight per cent of those under 18 discharged from prison in 2004 are reconvicted within one year. Seventy-five per cent of discharged 18–20 year olds are reconvicted within two years.

However, according to recent statistics, adult re-offending rates have fallen significantly. Adult re-offences fell 13 per cent between 2005 and 2006 – against the target of a ten per cent fall between 2005 and 2011 – from just under 168 re-offences per 100 offenders to just over 146. These figures are set against a

---

[22] Edghill (2008).

[23] Social Exclusion Unit (2002).

[24] The Scottish Executive set itself the target of reducing the reconviction rate by two per cent by March 2008.

significant long-term decline, with the frequency of adult re-offending falling 22.9 per cent between 2000 and 2006.[25]

Reconviction rates decrease by age: 54 per cent of those under 21 were reconvicted within two years, compared with 35 per cent of those over 30. This signals an important pattern, where most young men grow out of crime during their twenties. This does not mean their behaviour is an acceptable way of growing up. What could be done to prevent this behaviour in the first place? But also, what is available to help them move beyond it, more quickly and more effectively – 'knocking young offenders off the crime escalator'? An effective response means tailoring provision of learning opportunities to the relevant age and stage of the offender.

2.3 The educational profile

Arguably the single most outstanding feature of the prison population is its lack of education and skills. All the figures point in the same direction. Half of all prisoners do not have the skills required by 96 per cent of jobs. Forty-three per cent have a reading level at or below that expected of an 11 year old; the figure for writing is 82 per cent. Only one in five can complete a job application form.[26]

Figure 2: Educational backgrounds of prisoners[27]

Category	General population	Prisoners
No qualifications	15	52
Reading below Level 1	16	37
Excluded from school	3	49
Regular truant	4	30

■ General population   ■ Prisoners

Note: Literacy Level 1 is broadly equivalent to the level of skill expected of a competent 11 year old.

---

[25] Prison Service News 261.
[26] All figures from the Prison Reform Trust website, http://www.prisonreformtrust.org.uk/.
[27] Source: National Audit Office (2008).

Twenty to thirty per cent of prisoners have learning disabilities or difficulties that interfere with their ability to cope within the criminal justice system. They are at risk of re-offending because of unidentified needs and consequent lack of support or services, and are unlikely to benefit from programmes designed to address offending behaviour.[28]

The education system has not succeeded with the vast majority of offenders. (To be clear, this is not the responsibility of the education system alone.) It is not just the absolute low levels which matter. The disparities are significant in themselves. Area-based analysis of juvenile crime has revealed that growing educational inequality is associated with rises in convictions, and also with the numbers of racially motivated crimes (though not with property offences).[29]

A recent longitudinal study reports that:

> "Prisoners tended to prioritise employment and skills deficits over health and family problems in terms of the help they wanted during the course of their sentence. Nearly half (48 per cent) of the sample reported needing help finding employment. Help getting qualifications and improving work-related skills were reported by 42 per cent and 41 per cent respectively."[30]

A contribution from one of the participants in the IFLL seminar, from the Shannon Trust, summed up the challenge thus:

> "In school or in later life these failures are hard to rectify. Prison offers them the best chance they will have to put it right. There is the time and the lack of distractions."

But does the system genuinely offer the opportunity?

---

[28] Talbot (2009).
[29] Sabates et al (2008).
[30] Stewart (2008).

iFLL
Inquiry into the Future
for Lifelong Learning

3. Offender learning

The core education and training provision for offenders has three main components: in England and Wales, the Offenders Learning and Skills Service (OLASS); the learning which occurs in prison workshops, funded by HMPS; and Offender Behaviour and Resettlement courses (OBRs), funded by the prison service and provided by prisons and a range of voluntary organisations.[31] In addition, the Open University caters for about 1,200 prisoners, funded by the Department for Business, Innovation and Skills (BIS) and the Open University. The picture is further complicated, both by devolutionary diversity, and because we should not confuse size with significance: there are many small but important forms of provision in the voluntary sector.

The service is in a period of transition. There have been a number of critical reports highlighting deficiencies, but improvements have also been noted. For example, offender learning was identified by Ofsted as the least effective of all learning and skills sectors, with 24 per cent of provision inadequate; but this is a significant advance on the previous inspection, where the figure was one-third.

As a recent Ministry of Justice report concludes:

> "Most sentenced prisoners serve less than a year in custody, and have limited time and opportunity to engage with prison programmes. The findings illustrate the difficult decisions faced by offender managers, and those involved in the sentence planning and induction processes, who have to prioritise interventions and resettlement support according to individuals' needs. Rigorous assessment of prisoners' needs on reception is therefore essential."[32]

Two recent Ofsted reports stressed the need for clear national strategies for supporting the different learning needs of long and short-term offenders. They highlight the fact that there are no national guidelines for learning and skills programmes that relate to the amount of time offenders spend in prisons (Ofsted, 2009a and 2009b).

---

[31] In April 2005, The Scottish Prison Service procured a new learning, skills and employability (LSE) service to replace the previous education service contracts delivered in all public sector prisons. A key goal of the LSE contracts is to ensure that appropriate education and training is provided so that offenders can improve their opportunities of engaging in fulfilling and sustainable employment, learning or training following their release. The contracts were awarded to two further education colleges, Motherwell College and Carnegie College. There are also private education providers involved in delivering a core curriculum built round five skills.

[32] Stewart (2008), p. iii.

3.1 OLASS

OLASS's main stakeholders are the Department for Business, Innovation and Skills (BIS),[33] the Department for Children, Schools and Families (DCSF), the Ministry of Justice and the Department for Work and Pensions (DWP). OLASS is currently managed by the Learning and Skills Council (LSC) on behalf of BIS, although this will change when the LSC disappears and the arrangements governing the new Skills Funding Agency come into effect (responsibility for young offenders will be split off and given to local authorities). It awards contracts to around 25 providers, which currently includes both FE colleges and commercial providers. Operationally, the National Offender Management Service (NOMS) is also involved, along with the Youth Justice Board, Jobcentre Plus and the Connexions Service. NOMS brings together prison and probation functions and seeks to provide 'end-to-end offender management'. Education, training and employment is one of the seven 'pathways' identified in the National Reducing Re-offending Action Plan.

The budget for OLASS is £129 million. In 2002–03 an average of £1,185 per prisoner was spent on education in custody – less than half the cost of secondary school per student education. However, government spending on prison education doubled between 1999–2000 and 2004–05, and has continued to grow (see Figure 3).

Figure 3: Spend on offender learning and skills since 2004–05[34]

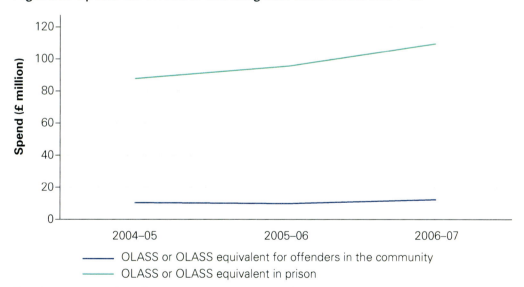

The investment in offender learning is therefore growing, but current expenditure on OLASS is under three per cent of the total prison budget of £4.3 billion.

At any one time, around a third of the prison population is involved in some way in education classes. In his evidence to the Public Accounts Committee, Mark Haysom,

---

[33] As this report went to press, government reorganisation led to the disappearance of DIUS, with most of its functions being subsumed into a new department: Business, Innovation and Skills (BIS).
[34] Source: National Audit Office.

Chief Executive of the LSC, reported:

> "82,290 learners engaged with learning at that time. That represents 53
> per cent of the total number of prisoners that were in custody during that
> year. We know that we are growing the numbers of people engaged so
> we know on an average monthly basis that, prior to the Learning and Skills
> Service, about 30 per cent of offenders were engaging. In the first year of
> the Service that grew to 36 per cent and is now running at 38 per cent." [35]

In 2006–07 the average annual teaching hours allocated per prisoner were around
30. The great bulk of provision is focused on basic skills. The teaching time is tiny –
especially given that offenders have one thing in abundance and that is time – and the
curricular range looks very imbalanced.

OLASS is still in transition/development, with the handover to the LSC still relatively
recent, and further structural change impending. Tensions arise from the way it
answers to different stakeholders (see *Appendix A*). It received a recent report from
the Parliamentary Accounts Committee (PAC), whose conclusions are summarised
below. These are harsh given that it is still early days for the new service, but deserve
quoting. It is notable that 28 per cent of courses in prisons go uncompleted, costing
up to £30 million. According to a recent study, the biggest reason for not completing a
course was being moved to another prison.[36]

PAC report on OLASS: key conclusions[37]

The delivery partners – DIUS, LSC, NOMS – are not working adequately in
partnership.

Provision for short-sentence prisoners is not worked out.

Quality of learning plans is poor.

Lack of core curriculum.

Inadequate recording, tracking of progress and monitoring of employment
outcome.

The position in other parts of the UK is somewhat different. Scotland is in the process
of a radical reform of its criminal justice system, following the 2005 Management
of Offenders Act. This establishes Criminal Justice Authorities to bring all agencies
together to provide services built round the offender. A new National Advisory Body
will shape long-term strategy to reduce re-offending and the harm caused.

---

[35] Public Accounts Committee: Forty-seventh Report of Session 2007–08 Evidence. Q7, p.22:
http://www.parliament.the-stationery-office.com/pa/cm200708/cmselect/cmpubacc/584/584.pdf
[36] Prisoners' Education Trust, Inside Time and RBE Consultancy (2009).
[37] Source: House of Commons (2008).

3.2 Prison and workplace training

Preparing offenders for work is a major task of the prison system, just as training and retraining people for work is a major function of the education system. However, work in prison is mostly not conducive to skill development and use. It is usually fragmented, repetitive and menial. 'Many workshops in Britain's increasingly overcrowded prisons resemble nothing more than industrial museums.'[38] Elsewhere in the Inquiry we refer to expansive and restricted workplaces; i.e. those which encourage and discourage learning.[39] Prison work is at the latter, highly restricted, end of the spectrum.

Just as importantly, work in prison is not treated as work is in society outside. It is not properly paid, and not recognised as employment. The Howard League for Penal Reform[40] argues strongly for giving offenders work that is more closely identified with work outside, since prisoners currently pay no tax or National Insurance, prisons reinforce the legitimacy of 'cash in hand', and the wages are so low that it reinforces the notion that crime pays better than work.

The benefits from proper work with a proper wage would be numerous. It would enable prisoners to contribute to their families and to restorative justice; it would help the atmosphere in prison; and it would, above all, give them a better chance of gaining employment outside.

The Barbed initiative was a graphic design social enterprise launched by the Howard League for Penal Reform (HLPR) in 2005. The aims were to provide a high-quality graphic design service, whilst providing an innovative approach to prisoners' work. It recruited 11 prisoners as employees, on the same type of contract as other HLPR staff. To imitate payments for transport, food etc, prisoners paid 30 per cent of their wages into a fund supporting projects such as the Prison Education Trust, as well as paying tax. However, there were tensions between the Prison Service and the employer, and HM Revenue and Customs deemed that prisoners may not be legally taxed. The Barbed initiative has now ceased, at least provisionally.[41]

---

[38] Progress Policy Group (2008).
[39] Williams and Wilson (2009, forthcoming).
[40] Howard League for Penal Reform. *Work in Prisons*. Briefing for Rt Hon. David Hanson MP.
[41] See Green (2008).

IFLL
Inquiry into the Future
for Lifelong Learning

3.3 Distance learning

It seems obvious that distance learning should be a major means of allowing prisoners to transcend the physical barrier of imprisonment. It should also offer opportunities in a form which allows offenders to make use of a commodity they have in abundance: time.

The Prisoners' Education Trust (PET) estimates that at least 4,000 prisoners are studying by distance learning. PET itself funds over 2,000 prisoners each year to take distance learning courses in over 200 subject areas, with the majority of courses focused on vocational paths and gaining employment. Distance learning, along with e-learning, is a recognised element in the OLASS policy document, *The Offender Learning Journey*, yet distance learning is not available other than to a tiny minority or through charitable funding. When asked what kind of support would be most helpful to their learning, the majority of prisoners say that internet access is the top priority. Distance learning can greatly enhance prisoners' employability by adding specific and often highly vocational skills and knowledge to their basic qualifications.

The major single provider of distance learning opportunities is the Open University (OU). There are over 1,000 prisoners studying with the OU. However, as PET has noted:

> "Apart from pilot projects operating in a handful of prisons, there is no access to email or the internet for prisoners. In relation to distance learning, this means that prisoners cannot study the majority of OU courses, since they require internet access; they cannot read extra material or do research related to their courses. This limitation makes contact with tutors slow and cumbersome as it must largely be done by post. It means that some courses with online exams cannot be completed, even if all the coursework has been paper-based and completed successfully." [42]

There are other distance learning providers besides the OU. Learndirect enables secure Internet-based provision in around 25 prisons, reaching nearly 3,000 learners.[43] It demonstrates that prison can be reconciled with internet access. The Learndirect pilot project funded by the European Social Fund, involving 20 prisons, ran from January 2005 to December 2006 and provided access to a portfolio of over 400 Learndirect courses as well as online tests and examinations. The evaluation concluded that 'e-learning is an engaging and attractive way to deliver education to offenders in both custody and the community'. Evidence to the Inquiry suggests that recruitment of qualified staff is an issue, as well as the more general problem of ICT availability.

---

[42] http://www.prisonerseducation.org.uk/fileadmin/user_upload/doc/offender_learning_matters/ICT_for_Prisoner_Learning._Feb._2009.pdf
[43] See Powell (2008a, 2008b); Betson (2008).

IFLL
Inquiry into the Future
for Lifelong Learning

Two examples of provision

Polaris: A Ministry of Justice pilot project, Polaris, has been developed in seven London prisons. Each of the prisons has a Polaris room with a number of computers which have limited access to a number of websites that have been 'white-listed'. The sites, which are accessible through this system, have been security checked and unacceptable links have been removed. Prisoners who wish to use Polaris are risk assessed and have access for timed sessions, under supervision. However, there is no funding for this project from the start of the next financial year.

Virtual Campus: The LSC/OLASS is running a pilot project where an online 'virtual campus' is being made available in prisons for use by individual prisoners under supervision. The virtual campus enables access to a range of information sources and some websites which have been security checked and stripped of hyperlinks. It includes some interactive processes; prisoners can use it to develop a CV and make applications for jobs, for example. The virtual campus is currently being trialled in two English regions. One prison in each region is live, Swinfen Hall and Blundeston, and plans exist to extend it quickly across the two regions and across the whole prison estate over the next five years. The virtual campus includes access to Learndirect.

Other distance learning technologies may be more traditional, but none the less effective for all that. One example is prison radio, which is a way of enabling offenders to learn and at the same time retain contact with their children.[44]

3.4 Specific programmes

There are many other programmes which provide for offenders and related learners. These are far too numerous to summarise here. Instead, we provide a list of examples to indicate the range of relevant initiatives, drawn mainly from evidence submitted to the Inquiry. They are selected because they address the key issues identified elsewhere, and illustrate good practice.

Family learning

Family learning takes place in a number of prisons, including, but not restricted to, women's prisons. In London, one programme is delivered by South Bank University and funded by the LSC.[45] This brings together prisoners and some of the 150,000

[44] See Tilley (2008).
[45] See Savitzky (2008).

children who have parents in prison. It provides a structure and context for family visits, for example doing homework together, with a positive outcome.

"It's nice to be able to do something creative with my mum. It makes us closer to each other, sharing this time."

(Child visitor, Holloway)

Related initiatives include:

- Safe Ground's Family Man programme. The objective of Family Man is to make prisoners more active members of their family while in prison. The skills and confidence they acquire during the course help them engage, not just with their family, but also with the prison system itself. Lasting an intensive 75 hours, Family Man uses drama techniques to engage large groups of learners of mixed ability. The finale is a presentation that allows the students to show off their new knowledge and skills to a wider audience. This spreads awareness among other prisoners and also internal and external agents. Over 600 prisoners and staff from 12 establishments have brought this course to life;[46]

- Storybook Dads. Prisoners are recorded telling a story with the use of a microphone and a minidisk recorder. The story is downloaded onto a computer and any mistakes are edited out. Music and sound effects are added (from a database of many hundreds) and the final story is put onto a CD. Poor readers (or even non-readers) are not excluded from the scheme. Since the scheme's inception in 2002 over 1,700 prisoners have participated.[47]

Tackling substance abuse

Kent Drugs and Alcohol Team Certificate in Community Justice is a Level 3 City & Guilds qualification.[48] The programme provides a pathway into education, training and volunteering/employment, including ex-service users, some of whom are themselves ex-offenders. It thus enables experience of abuse to be turned to positive use. It is a 'practice-based qualification'. It is run in an FE college, demonstrating the distinctive inclusiveness of the college sector.[49]

Other examples of programmes in this field include:

- Rehabilitation for Addicted Prisoners Trust (RAPT), which provides services to over 13,000 people every year within the criminal justice system: in prisons, intensive drug rehabilitation programmes; and in the community, pioneering treatment and aftercare for offenders, ex-offenders, and people referred from outside the criminal justice system;[50]

---

[46] See www.safeground.org.uk/courses_familyman.php
[47] See www.storybookdads.co.uk
[48] Duncan (2008).
[49] For information on this more generally, see Howard (2009).
[50] See www.rapt.org.uk/

- Counselling, Assessment, Referral, Advice and Throughcare Services (CARATS), which provides initial assessment following referral; advice to prisoners with substance misuse problems; liaison with healthcare, both in prison and in the community; care plan assessments; one-to-one counselling and groupwork services; assessment for intensive treatment programmes in prison; and throughcare linking with community drug treatment services ensuring, where required, prisoners are offered post-release support for up to eight weeks.[51]

Financial capability

Money issues have been identified by NOMS as one of the causes of re-offending and therefore access to advice and money education training are important services. Forty-eight per cent of prisoners have a history of debt and 60 per cent are financially excluded (i.e. do not have access to mainstream financial products such as bank accounts).

Credit Action is working in partnership with the Co-operative Group to produce and distribute basic financial education materials for use within prisons. Financial capability is also one of the areas addressed by Unlock, the national association of reformed offenders, in its major programme to reduce reoffending rates.[52] Staff in 33 prisons have been trained to deliver financial capability, as well as in several charities and community groups.

This is all the more salient since financial capability is one of the core capabilities identified more generally by the Inquiry, along with health and civic capabilities – both equally relevant to offender learning.

Dyslexia and reading skills

Many prisoners have learning disabilities, of various kinds. The Touch Type programme provides training for dyslexic prisoners.[53] The aim is to provide continuity once prisoners have left; and because dyslexia runs in families, to extend the service to their children, breaking the cycle of disadvantage. The programme has also enabled prison officers to identify their own needs. Another example of a programme for dyslexics is found at South Thames College.[54]

---

[51] See http://pso.hmprisonservice.gov.uk/PSO_3630_carats.doc
[52] See www.unlock.org.uk
[53] See Freeman (2008).
[54] See Alston and Starrs (2008).

IFLL
Inquiry into the Future
for Lifelong Learning

'Toe by Toe' reading scheme

'The single best thing introduced into prisons in the last ten years.' That's how Stephen Shaw, Prison and Probation Ombudsman, describes the Shannon Trust's 'Toe by Toe' reading scheme. Now rolling out a new Reading Network in the West Midlands Young Offender estate, the charity is helping to reshape offenders' prospects. The Shannon Trust was set up eight years ago specifically to work with people in custody, teaching prisoner mentors to teach fellow offenders to read. The trust enables prisons to deliver the Toe by Toe reading manual, developed and written by Keda Cowling after 20 years of working with children with dyslexia and reading difficulties. It breaks reading down into a series of small, simple sounds helping people to learn, not just step by step, but 'Toe by Toe'. It has also been designed so anyone with a moderate reading ability will be able to use it to teach others to read, which works well in prisons. (Source: *Prison Service News 261*, Sept/Oct 2008)

Early preventive action

North Yorkshire library enables young offenders to conduct research on 19th century prisons, gaining a new perspective as well as confidence in their abilities. The same library reaches out to young children (aged 8–13) identified as at risk, helping them to use the library to research local issues.[55]

Community-based adult education in Derbyshire delivers Construction Training for young males, many of whom have been involved with petty crime. The 'soft' learning outcomes are:

- it motivates individuals to get out of bed in the morning;
- it encourages working as a team;
- it encourages persistence and completion.[56]

3.5 Workforce capability: Staff development for prison officers

A key condition for a successful strategy on offender learning is the commitment and competence of the prison staff.[57] Prison staff often themselves have low qualifications and low skills, but efforts are being made to improve this. The HM Prison Service (HMPS) published its strategy for professionalising the Prison Service in 2007, recognising that all staff need to access continuing professional development (see box below). Newcastle College provides an NVQ in Custodial Care. Since 2007, Level

---

[55] See Sweetmore (2008); Hooper (2008).
[56] See Javanaud (2008).
[57] See Braggins and Talbot (2005).

3 is undertaken by all new prison officers, with 2,100 undertaken per year. NIACE is working with HMPS to develop their capacity, especially on basic skills.[58] South Bank University's LLU+ unit delivers professional development across London's prison and probation service, bridging service divides and improving the quality of OLASS provision.

Training – qualifying on the job

The new nationally-accredited Custodial Care NVQ is split into two levels. The NVQ Level 2 is a voluntary qualification aimed at Operational Support Grades who wish to become prison officers. Since September 2007, all new prison officers have to complete the Level 3 NVQ during their first 12 months on the job. So far, 50 assessors have been appointed by Newcastle College, which acts as the administrative hub of the NVQ, and this number is likely to increase as more candidates join the scheme.

From 2009, prison officers who may have been in the Prison Service for years will also get the chance to take the Level 3 NVQ if they wish. While not obligatory, this is a positive move designed to enhance career progression and boost professional confidence. The intention is that having a nationally-recognised qualification will give the job greater kudos for potential recruits and the reassurance that once they join there is a structured career path to follow. (Source: *Prison Service News 257, Jan/Feb 2008*)

Raising awareness of women's issues

The first pilot of a programme designed to promote issues surrounding women prisoners to staff is underway at HMP Send. Launched by Maria Eagle, Ministerial Champion for Women in the Criminal Justice System, the Women Awareness Staff Programme (WASP) is a women-specific programme designed to complement what new staff will have learnt on Prison Officer Entry Level Training (POELT). Running as a two-day programme, the course will include modules on the background to women offending, female behaviour in custody and conflict resolution. (Source: *Prison Service News* 260, July/Oct 2008)

In addition to the professional prison staff, prisoners themselves have the capability to take on volunteer roles and make a real contribution to better support and provision. As the Prisoners' Education Trust (PET) notes in its submission to the chairman of the Public Accounts Committee report on offender learning: [59]

---

[58] NIACE/HMPS (2008).
[59] National Audit Office (2008).

"In relation to learning, they currently act as classroom assistants, peer advisers, learning and skills representatives and learning mentors. Other roles could be added. This kind of activity has a double value; both extending provision, and adding a further valuable level of learning and potential reform for the volunteer prisoners concerned."

Drawing on and respecting the experience of reformed offenders is a guiding principle of Unlock, which stresses the contribution this can make to helping others to leave crime behind.

4. Framing and evaluating the relationship between offending and learning

The array of provision indicated above illustrates clearly the challenge involved in attempting to estimate the actual and potential value of learning in relation to offending. This section does no more than indicate the parameters involved. As a recent major report on mental health and prison commented:

> "Cost-benefit analysis can be defined as a systematic attempt to identify, value and compare all the costs and all the benefits of alternative policies or interventions. The value-for-money case for diversion is not just or even mainly about achieving narrowly defined financial benefits such as cost savings in the criminal justice system or elsewhere in the public sector. The Exchequer or taxpayer perspective is certainly important but is only part of the story."[60]

John Bynner's IFLL Public Value Paper on a life-course perspective on learning and crime explores these methodological issues in some detail.[61]

We need to emphasise two points at the outset. First, because it is individuals that learn, the whole argument around the contribution lifelong learning can make to crime and social exclusion is often seen as a matter of individual agency, of enhancing people's personal capacities, but also their personal responsibility. The linear rationalist model runs as follows: that as people learn more they will: a) have more opportunities to lead a gainful and lawful life; b) realise that they have these opportunities; and c) be more socialised so that, d) they will choose to exploit these opportunities in preference to criminal or other anti-social behaviour. But this is not the way the world works, at least for the most part – any more than stiffer sentences deter by causing offenders to reflect and then duly desist. We should not believe that learning has its effects purely by changing individual attitudes and behaviour, and we certainly cannot see this as the royal route to solving the problems of crime and social exclusion.

Secondly, therefore, if lifelong learning is to help in tackling crime and social exclusion, the learning concerned is not only that of offenders or potential offenders. We are all party to the way in which our society handles crime and punishment. There are imaginative schemes and initiatives which tackle the issues and which both require learning and generate it. Family learning is a good example, which among other things can help parents acquire skills and confidence to exercise appropriate authority with their children. Certainly, restorative justice procedures aim for change in offender behaviour. But they also entail learning and development in the other participants, at many levels: from the technical skills involved in managing such processes to deeper

---

[60] Sainsbury Centre (2009a).
[61] Bynner (2009).

IFLL
Inquiry into the Future
for Lifelong Learning

personal development such as is involved in understanding and forgiveness. Processes such as these show how wrong it is to treat learning as a matter of isolated individual change. In short, although this paper deals primarily with offenders, there are much wider issues caught up in the web of relationships between lifelong learning and the crime theme.

Any comprehensive assessment would need to encompass three different levels. First, there is the extent to which raising *general levels of education* can be expected to have an effect on crime and anti-social behaviour, and the way these are handled. The second level deals with *different types of learning and achievement*: vocational, academic, certificated, uncertificated and so on, at different levels. Some subjects or areas of study may have a particular effect; it would, for example, be worth debating whether drama, ethics or sociology has the most positive impact on people's social outlook and behaviour. If the goal is to strengthen learning's impact on crime, we need to enhance access to the most effective types of learning, rather than assume that a general uplift will do the trick.

The third level is that of *specific interventions* aimed at reducing or preventing offending behaviour. These may be designed for groups which have already engaged in criminal activity, or for at-risk groups, even quite early on.[62] Even where interventions are specifically designed to address offending behaviour, it is difficult to evaluate them with a high degree of certainty. A recent report on diverting people with mental health problems addresses the issue in terms which apply generally:

> "Routinely collected information on outcomes and effectiveness is largely non-existent and in consequence all schemes find it difficult to evaluate their success."[63]

Of course, action – innovation, improvement, policy – is needed at all three levels. The actual and potential contribution of lifelong learning to reducing crime and social exclusion can only be understood if all of these are taken into account.

The focus here is more on offenders and those considered likely to offend, and therefore towards the instrumental end of the spectrum. This is because it is easier (though still not easy) to identify causal links between learning and lower crime rates at these levels, and because it opens up more practical policy options. But this does not for one moment mean that education's general role is less important than the others.

There is space here just to sketch in fragments of the picture. Improving basic skills is a central challenge which addresses the very large proportion of the offender population who lack them, so that this is identified as a, or even *the*, priority area for action, and is currently the primary focus of educational efforts for offenders.[64] The SEU report in 2002 found that basic skills learning can contribute to a reduction in

---

[62] See Sweetmore (2008) and Hooper (2008), on outreach to at-risk 8–13 year olds.
[63] Sainsbury Centre (2009a).
[64] See Bynner (2009).

reoffending of about 12 per cent. This result in itself could be translated into costs and benefits, using some of the figures in Section 2. Obviously a 12 per cent reduction in re-offending yields a far lower overall saving, since there are fixed costs. But at £40,000 a year in average prisoner costs, even on fairly modest assumptions about how far it translates into savings, a reduction of this size will yield very substantial benefits, given the high proportion of prisoners who lack basic skills.

Achieving some learning gains leads to further learning. Subsequent research following up prisoners after release shows that levels of literacy and numeracy improved after training, especially for prisoners who received at least 30 hours basic skills training. However, there was no strong direct link between this and getting a job; of those who had got a job, this was not associated with achieving Level 1 skills, but more often due to connections through family or friends. Self-reported offending was less common among those who have achieved Level 1, but not at a statistically significant level.[65]

The point about family and friends is crucial, underlining the importance of social capital. Education and training alone will not do the trick. Their impact depends on other factors. But in turn, offenders' learning can impact positively on their relations with family and friends, and help them keep the kind of company which has an interest in preventing them from re-offending rather than the reverse.

Increasingly, it is obvious that approaches must be holistic, dealing with accommodation, employment, training and health together, and recognising that the (ex-)offender exists in a social context. As a recent Ministry of Justice research summary observes:

> "There is also a growing consensus that broader, multi-modal approaches, going beyond individual interventions, are what work best."[66]

A range of approaches to evaluation need to be developed, narrow and broad, and with different criteria. One attempt to cost the effect of desistance is made in one of the IFLL Public Value Papers.[67] This applies very stringent, narrowly defined standards of evidence, and is therefore forced to use data from experimental designs in the US. It includes a range of costs, and attempts to estimate the cumulative savings from effective interventions which flow over a lifetime. It shows that the returns to training interventions, even with only partial success in preventing recidivism, are high when compared with the costs of offenders continuing on their previous paths. Different levels of cost are considered: the direct ones alone, then the costs to victims (lost productivity, pain and suffering, lost property). The variance in the results is predictably great, because of the diversity of the studies and methodologies, but a reasonably conservative estimate of the saving from lower reoffending which could be expected to flow from investing in in-prison educational and vocational interventions is around £0.5 billion for a given cohort.

---

[65] Chitty, Ministry of Justice (2008).
[66] May, Sharma and Stewart (2009).
[67] Matrix Knowledge Group (2009).

Figure 4: Total savings per offender as a result of re-offending and intervention costs[68]

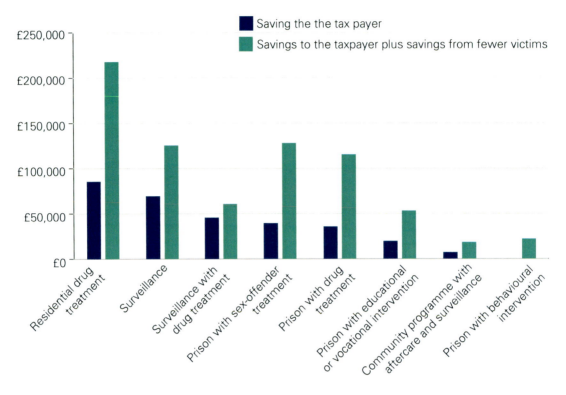

A slightly broader study[69] compared interventions which include educational or vocational components to prison on its own, as well as to other interventions which concentrate, for example, only on drug addictions. The costs are high, averaging around £27,000 per offender per year. But the returns are higher: taking into account the 15 per cent reduction in the likelihood of reoffending, the net saving to the taxpayer worked out at nearly £19,000; adding on estimated victim costs increased this figure more than threefold. The assumptions for these kinds of study are necessarily quite large, and the potential variance big, so these figures must be treated with caution; but the direction is clear.

[68] Source: Matrix Knowledge Group (2007).
[69] Matrix Knowledge Group (2007).

Prison with educational or vocational intervention

Programmes included basic education, prison-based vocational training and support with finding employment post-release. Also included were prison industry employment and/or training.

Evidence base

Six studies met the selection criteria. They included 7,623 individuals.

Effectiveness at reducing re-offending, compared to prison

Based on this evidence, offenders receiving educational or vocational interventions whilst in prison are 15 per cent less likely to re-offend after release than comparable offenders receiving only prison sentences.

Cost of intervention

£27,109 per offender per year.

Value for money compared to prison per offender

The following figures show the estimated value for money from using this intervention instead of prison. They are based on the reduced chance of re-offending (taking into account of the cost of the intervention) over an offender's post-release lifetime.

Saving to the taxpayer	£18,858
Saving to the taxpayer plus the saving from fewer victim costs	£67,226

However, not all analysis of costs and benefits can be quantified in this way. Very different types of evidence come from initiatives such as Arts in Prison and many other projects.[70] Thus, evidence from work at the University of Central Lancashire focuses on the arts as a route to self-expression and an expanded communicative range, which can be transformational in itself. Most studies point to enhanced self-esteem, confidence and transferable skills, but the observations are superficial and over-generalised.

> "There is a need for in-depth ethnographic studies of learning in situ to understand the more subtle details of mechanism and effect, and especially for longitudinal studies of long-term effects."[71]

---

[70] See the Anne Peaker Centre for Arts in Criminal Justice at http://www.apcentre.org.uk/civicrm/event/info?reset=1&id=12
[71] Personal communication from Professor Lynn Froggett of UCL.

Inquiry into the Future
for Lifelong Learning

In short, we need variety both in the methods used to make evaluations, and in the criteria applied – what kinds of benefit we expect or hope for, and what 'currency' we use for measuring them. Both the investments and the benefits can be estimated at different levels of precision. On the benefits side, some will be able to have pound signs attached to them; others will not, but still need to be brought into the equation. Above all, we need horizons which extend sufficiently to allow the true lifetime costs and benefits to be evaluated. There is much more out there to be drawn out but the knowledge base is still fragmentary.[72] In addition, as the Sainsbury Centre report suggested, we need stronger communication and exchange between different approaches to estimating benefits.

---

[72] See Bynner (2009).

5. Conclusion

The conclusions below relate the above analysis to wider discussion within the Inquiry.

5.1 Boosting human capital

The strongest consensus is around the need to improve the skills of those in prison, to give them a reasonable chance of desisting. Progress has been made on this in recent years. Much more remains to be done, on volume and quality. A major emphasis on basic skills is correct, but should not dominate, and basic skills should be *embedded* in a wider curriculum. The possibility of *progression* through different levels is important; so is the breadth of offer (see Section 5.5 and 5.8). A *unit-based credit system* generally (i.e. for the country, not just in respect of offender education) would be a major step forward.

Skills are not the same as qualifications, as the House of Commons Select Committee recently commented in relation to the Leitch Report. Given the poor educational background of many offenders, testing and certification may be inappropriate, reducing motivation and success. *Stronger support for provision which is not necessarily accredited* is an important part of expanding the supply side. This is especially the case in areas of innovation, where voluntary organisations have played a demonstrable major role. In particular, voluntary organisations can draw on a wide range of relevant experience, with greater flexibility and more tailored goals than is often possible in the formal sector.

5.2 Increasing social capital: networks and family learning

For lifelong learning to have a reasonable chance of improving the crime situation, offenders need to be part of networks and social groups which will support their desistance – and not the reverse. The family is the essential unit here. Imprisonment of a family member puts family and other social links under enormous pressure. We have referred above to some of the imaginative schemes which exist to maintain these links. Learning is a way of helping this happen, and of increasing the offender's motivation to desist. Social links are also often a prime route into employment. Without social capital, human capital often goes unused.

But family learning is not appropriate for all, since many offenders lack family connections. Strengthening peer support, and helping to form links with supportive external networks, would boost their chances of sustained success.

Partnership is an overworked term, but it has particular salience in this context. Most obviously, there is a need for still stronger partnerships between the prison and probation services, voluntary organisations and colleges, to secure the best provision

Inquiry into the Future
for Lifelong Learning

and to ensure continuity in the learning journeys. Of course, there are important issues of security and accountability which cannot be ignored, but this is an area where the voluntary sector has shown itself to be particularly innovative, maybe through force of circumstance, and this needs to be facilitated.

5.3 Strengthening personal identity: well-being and mental health

Lifelong learning can have very positive effects on mental health.[73] It boosts self-esteem, and it provides people with social contacts and a purpose to their days and lives, in addition to the skills, knowledge and competences that come from learning. However, the mental health challenges of the current prison situation are beyond the levels where most lifelong learning can make a difference. It is abundantly clear that many of the people who reach prison have mental health problems which mean that they should not be there.

One consequence is that they stand little chance of being successfully treated. Their presence in such large numbers also means that educational interventions for genuine offenders have reduced chance of succeeding. So the argument for *early diversion into appropriate health and psychiatric services* is very strong.

However, even for offenders who do not have mental health problems so serious that they should be catered for by health services rather than prison, the need will still be there for educational approaches which take a *whole-person approach*. It is pointless attempting to build up someone's human capital if their self-confidence and sense of identity are in fragments.

5.4 Young people and identity

'Young people have no place they need to be, so no one misses them.'[74] People disappear into prisons. They are not only physically invisible; they have no official existence, other than as a prison number. They are not citizens, since they cannot vote. They may earn a small amount of money, but have no tax code and do not pay taxes. Over half of those entering prison are not registered with a GP. Many, especially the younger ones, have not even a driving licence as an official document. The prison is their address. They therefore have no identity, other than as a prisoner, and no symbolic stake in the institutions which define most of us. For young men in particular, who make up a large part of the prison population, this is in striking contrast to many of their contemporaries. These may either be students, and therefore part of institutions specifically designed to develop their capacities and which gives them identity and official recognition; or/and members of the workforce, who have made the

---

[73] See Field (2009).
[74] See Javanaud (2008).

transition into employment, who have an employment and tax record and the income to go with it.

The fact that they disappear physically is obviously part of the punishment involved in prison. But do they need to disappear so completely? As with so many issues in this theme, it goes well beyond questions of learning; but involvement in learning does something to counter this disappearance, as the small number registered with the OU would testify. Involvement in education and training can give people a sense of identity, with (an essential part of a secure identity) a sense of a future. *An Individual Learning Number* could symbolise this, even to a small extent. As suggested in the Progress Policy Group's support for a British version of the US Second Chance Act (SCA),[75] individuals could accumulate some form of credit towards an external qualification, and emerge with some stake already in the outside world. Payment of a proper minimum wage, with taxes and National Insurance deducted, could help them save towards this, as well as giving them the essential identity which others have.

5.5 Content/curriculum

The focus on basic skills in current offender education is understandable. The need is very prominent, and without these the employment prospects of ex-offenders are poor, and their chances of integration very reduced. However, it is worth asking just how far this focus should dominate. Rehabilitation and reintegration will often require complex learning with multiple objectives, designed to enable personal change as well as skill acquisition.

Basic skills should be embedded in wider learning. One implication is that more attention should be paid to *broader curricula* which are designed to foster and channel creativity. This does not mean the direct teaching of 'creativity', but provision which helps students to explore ways of developing through expressing themselves. This would allow offenders to strengthen their belief in their own ability to play a part in social and economic life, and to build their identity capital. It is 'soft' – but exactly in the sense of the soft skills, such as communication skills, which employers put at the head of their list.

5.6 Capabilities: financial, health, civic

The Inquiry is debating the range of capabilities which are in some measure essential to adults if they are to exercise control over their own lives. An initial core comprises financial, health and civic capabilities. All are relevant to this theme.

[75] The SCA supports coordinated initiatives whose target is to reduce recidivism by 50 per cent over a five-year period for offenders released from prison, jail, or a juvenile facility; see http://reentrypolicy.org/government_affairs/second_chance_act

Inquiry into the Future
for Lifelong Learning

Many offenders lack basic *financial* capability. They have debt problems, and/or beyond that do not have the necessary skills to manage their personal or household finances. This is an obvious fast track back into offending and prison.

Offenders are often in poor mental and physical *health*. Substance abuse is a particular issue, which spans both. Acquiring better ability to manage their own health needs – including learning to use health services to good effect – is for many an essential step in the reintegration process.

Prisoners are suspended from *civic* status. However, this need not deprive them of civic capabilities. The more these are sustained whilst they are in custody, the more likely they are to feel they have a stake in the outside world. It may enable them to turn their experience to good use, as with the Kent alcohol/drugs course.[76] The ability to deal with the criminal justice system is itself a form of civic capability. Twenty to thirty per cent of offenders have learning difficulties or disabilities that interfere with their ability to cope with the criminal justice system.

Organising a curriculum with these core capabilities in mind would be a big step forward.

5.7 The workforce: prison officer and probation staff as intermediaries, and offender volunteering

One of the outstanding issues to emerge from the Inquiry consultation on this theme was the need for better recruitment, and in particular better training for prison officers. Despite recent progress, the qualification requirements for these staff are low. Although data is lacking, a significant proportion themselves lack basic skills. It is wholly unreasonable to expect prison staff to promote learning opportunities for prisoners if they themselves do not have appropriate opportunities. Current efforts to improve staff capabilities need to make rapid progress, especially to meet the diverse and multiple profile of prisoners.

Both prison officers and probationers are prominent examples of potential 'intermediaries'. By this we mean professionals or volunteers who are not directly part of lifelong learning services, but who can play a crucial part in promoting learning. They can be guides, information sources and mentors. One example would be to ensure awareness in all prisons of schemes such as 'Toe by Toe', helping prisoners to teach fellow prisoners. Part of the enhanced staff training could be enabling them to play such an intermediary role effectively.[77]

A third aspect is the use of prisoners themselves as part of the lifelong learning workforce. Whatever their levels of formal education, offenders often have much to

---

[76] See Duncan (2008).

[77] An interesting example of the police acting as intermediaries was submitted as evidence from West Midlands police, where people brought to a police station under arrest are offered access to basic skills assessment and training, see Lee (2008).

give in the way of knowledge and skills, in a variety of roles: as classroom assistants, literacy tutors and mentors. This is a triple-win: the volunteers gain from doing the tutoring, the learners gain from an extended tutor workforce being available, and the rest of the population gains as a result.

5.8 ICT

Offenders in custody are a group for whom distance learning has particularly strong potential. It may not free them from place constraints, but it opens up a range of options which are otherwise by definition impossible. New technologies should enable access to a broad range of learning materials. However, this is currently very circumscribed, primarily through fears about giving prisoners open access to the internet.[78] OCR (Oxford, Cambridge and RSA Examinations) has produced a very sound set of strategic principles for the effective delivery of offender learning, which addresses this and other broader issues:

- IT facilities and internet access;
- integration of learning with other prison activities;
- relevant training and development for prison officers and other OLASS contributors;
- a service-wide database of transferable offender records; and
- incentives for offenders to participate in education.

Beyond these principles there is a myriad of possible developments. The Open University (OU) is likely to continue to be a central pillar for distance learning. But the OU's provision is complemented by a host of other initiatives which could be further developed; some of those already in play are referred to above. ICT can keep offenders in contact with the outside world, and reduce their reliance on other offenders as a peer group.

5.9 Transitions

The moment of coming out of prison is a critical phase in the path to reintegration. We heard strong signals that if an ex-offender does not find a secure base – accommodation, employment and/or an established training place – within just three weeks of coming out, any previous investment in education and training is likely to be completely wasted. The consequences can be literally fatal. In 2006 there were 382 suicides within one year of release from prison, a rate of 156 for 100,000, far higher than the general population; 20 per cent of these occured within the first 28 days. But even at lesser levels of failure, the costs to everyone are very high. It would be perverse to invest more in rehabilitation programmes and leave it to chance outside the gates.

[78] See Freeman (2008).

IFLL
Inquiry into the Future
for Lifelong Learning

This notion of key transition points chimes with other areas of the Inquiry's work, for example the transition from one level of education to another, or the transition from employment to retirement. These may be extended transitions or, as in the case with offenders, extremely abrupt ones. Investment should be strongly focused on enabling individuals to manage these key transitions as effectively as possible, if previous efforts are not to be wasted. The Inquiry's main report calls for an entitlement transition for offenders, guaranteeing them access to an education or training course immediately on their release, with suitable pre-release preparation and guidance.

5.10 The knowledge base

Crime is not unique in the challenge it poses in terms of establishing an adequate knowledge base to improve the contribution that lifelong learning can make to policy and practice.[79] Other themes such as poverty are equally broad and complex. Nevertheless, there are major problems in assembling a sound evidence base. For example, there is a very strong association between low basic skills and offending; yet evidence from the Ministry of Justice shows that low basic skills per se are actually a poor predictor of future offending or reoffending.[80] Establishing robust causal relationships, both on the origins of crime and on the effectiveness of educational approaches to its reduction, is very hard and often unrewarding.

One aspect is the standards which are set for 'evidence' to count. How far should quantitative evidence dominate, to the exclusion of qualitative or experiential? How far should we aspire to establish causality by rigorous but restricted methodology? As an example, one view is that there is no 'evidence' that moving offenders around between prisons, as happens frequently and disruptively, affects their educational achievements. Yet this is what is reported from the field, anecdotally but powerfully.[81] At what point does such 'evidence' pass the threshold in order to be given serious attention (which it now is)?

Understanding the complex causes of offending; designing appropriate education and training responses; and using good evaluation approaches – all these pose major challenges. Bridging research, policy and practice is an issue in education generally,[82] and this applies to offender learning just as much. Three things are needed:

---

[79] "There is evidence drawn from the wider population that improving individuals' basic literacy and numeracy skills increases the likelihood of them being in employment. There is little evidence, however, on the impact that learning kills provision in general, other than that which aims to improve basic skills, has in reducing re-offending, and the evidence base for the particular mix of learning and skills provision for offenders that will be most likely to achieve greater employability and reduce re-offending is poor." (National Audit Office, 2008).

[80] Chitty, Ministry of Justice (2008).

[81] "None of your stuff has followed you from one establishment to another, and so you come here and you're just a blank page again, so then you're waiting weeks and months to try and get on the courses that you'd already done in a different establishment! ... It's just like, what is the point?! ... That's more disheartening because you're told at one establishment: 'yeah, everything will be passed on to where you're going, so hopefully you should be able to just carry on where you left off'." Focus group member, offender at male training prison, (National Audit Office, 2008).

[82] See OECD (2007b).

- a life-course approach which sees the offender as changing over time, with particular needs at particular stages. Quantitative and qualitative longitudinal studies are especially valuable;

- an approach which understands the offender in his or her cultural and social context, and relates their potential and progress to the world outside; and

- a pluralism of method and a generosity of communication.[83]

From one angle it is not evidence that is missing, but practical initiative. As one submission argued:

> "Offender learning is a sector hallmarked by extensive research with clear findings followed by at best inconsistent and in some areas negligible action."[84]

It could be said that what is needed is a huge dose of concentrated common sense, to get effective measures in place before we go further down the hyper-incarceration road. But a good knowledge base would make a big difference.

---

[83] See Bynner (2009).
[84] See Brenchley (2008).

References

Braggins, J. and Talbot, J. (2005) *Wings of Learning: The role of the prison officer in supporting prisoner education.* London, The Centre for Crime and Justice Studies

Bynner, J. (2009) *Lifelong Learning and Crime: A Life-course Perspective: IFLL Public Value Paper 4.* Leicester, NIACE

Lord Carter's Review of Prisons (2007) *Securing The Future: Proposals for the efficient and sustainable use of custody in England and Wales.* London, House of Lords

Feinstein, L. (2002) *Quantitative Estimates of the Social Benefits of Learning 1: Crime. Research Report No. 5.* London, Centre for Research into the Wider Benefits of Learning

Field, J. (2009) *Well-being and Happiness: IFLL Thematic Paper 4.* Leicester, NIACE

Fryer, B. (forthcoming) *Citizenship, Belonging and Lifelong Learning: IFLL Thematic Paper 8.* Leicester, NIACE

Fullick, L. (2009) *Poverty Reduction and Lifelong Learning: IFLL Thematic Paper 6.* Leicester, NIACE

Green, P. (2008) *Prison work and social enterprise: the story of Barbed.* London, Howard League for Penal Reform

HM Inspectorate of Prisons (2004) *'No problems – old and quiet': Older prisoners in England and Wales. A thematic review by HM Chief Inspector of Prisons.* London, The Stationery Office

House of Commons (2008) *Meeting needs? The Offenders' Learning and Skills Service,* Committee of Public Accounts HC 584. London, The Stationery Office

Howard League for Penal Reform (2006) *Prison Information Bulletin 2: Women and girls in the penal system.* London, HLPR

Howard League for Penal Reform (2007) *Children in Prison.* London, HLPR

Karstedt, S. and Farrall, S. (2007) *Law Abiding Majority? The everyday crimes of the middle classes.* London, Centre for Crime and Justice Studies

Lochner, L. and Moretti, E. (2001) 'The Effect of Education on Crime: Evidence from Prison Inmates, Arrests and Self-Reports'. *National Bureau of Economic Research Working Paper,* 8605

Machin, S. and Meghir, C. (2000) 'Crime and Economic Incentives'. *The Institute for Fiscal Studies, Working Paper,* 00/17

Matrix Knowledge Group (2007) *The Economic Case For and Against Prison* http://www.matrixknowledge.co.uk/wp-content/uploads/the-economic-case-for-and-against-prison_web.pdf

Matrix Knowledge Group (2009) *Lifelong Learning and Crime: An Analysis of the Cost-effectiveness of In-prison Educational and Vocational Interventions: IFLL Public Value Paper 2*. Leicester, NIACE

Matrix Knowledge Group (2009) *Lifelong Learning and Well-being: An Analysis of the Relationship Between Adult Learning and Subjective Well-being: IFLL Public Value Paper 3*. Leicester, NIACE

Mauger, S. (2009) *Technological Change: IFLL Thematic Paper 2*. Leicester, NIACE

May, C., Sharma, N., and Stewart, D. (2009) *Factors linked to reoffending*. London, Ministry of Justice, Research Summary 5.

McNair, S. (2009a) *Demography and Lifelong Learning: IFLL Thematic Paper 1*. Leicester, NIACE

McNair, S. (2009b) *Migration, Communities and Lifelong Learning: IFLL Thematic Paper 3*. Leicester, NIACE

National Audit Office (2008) *Meeting needs? The Offenders' Learning and Skills Service*. London, NAO

NIACE/HMPS (2008) *HM Prison Service: Professionalising the Workforce*. Leicester, NIACE

OECD (2007a) *Understanding the Social Outcomes of Learning*. Paris, OECD Centre for Educational Research and Innovation

OECD (2007b) *Evidence in Education: Linking Research and Policy*. Paris, OECD Centre for Educational Research and Innovation.

Ofsted (2008) *The Annual Report of Her Majesty's Chief Inspector of Education, Children's Services and Skills 2007/08*. Available at: http://www.ofsted.gov.uk/Ofsted-home/Publications-and-research/Browse-all-by/Annual-Report/2007-08/The-Annual-Report-of-Her-Majesty-s-Chief-Inspector-2007-08

Ofsted (2009a and 2009b) *Learning and Skills for the longer-serving prisoner* and *An evaluation of the learning and skills provision for offenders serving short custodial sentences*. Both can be found on the Ofsted website: www.ofsted.gov.uk

Prisoners' Education Trust, Inside Time and RBE Consultancy (2009) *Brain Cells: Listening to prisoner learners*. London, Prisoners' Education Trust

Prison Reform Trust (2008) *Doing Time: The experiences and needs of older people in prison*. London, Prison Reform Trust

Prison Reform Trust (2009) *Too Little Too Late*. London, Prison Reform Trust

Progress Policy Group (2008) *Accountability, Prevention and Trust*. www.progressonline.org.uk

Sabates, R., et al (2008a) *Educational Inequality and Juvenile Crime: An Area Based Analysis*. London, WBL Centre Research Report 26

Sabates, R. (2008b) *The Impact of Lifelong Learning on Poverty Reduction: IFLL Public Value Paper 1*. Leicester, NIACE

Sainsbury Centre (2008a) *Short-changed: Spending on prison mental health care*. London, Sainsbury Centre for Mental Health

Sainsbury Centre (2008b) *On the outside: Continuity of care for people leaving prison*. London, Sainsbury Centre for Mental Health

Sainsbury Centre (2009) *Diversion: A better way for criminal justice and mental health*. London, Sainsbury Centre for Mental Health

Schuller, T., et al (2004) *The Benefits of Learning*. London, RoutledgeFalmer

Singleton, N., Meltzer, H. and Gatward, R. (1998) *Psychiatric Morbidity among Prisoners in England and Wales*. London, Office for National Statistics

Social Exclusion Unit (2002) *Reducing Re-Offending by Prisoners*, London, SEU.

Stewart, D. (2008) *The problems and needs of newly sentenced prisoners: results from a national survey*. Ministry of Justice Research Series 16/08

Talbot, J. (2009) *No One Knows*. London, Prison Reform Trust

Transform (2007) *After the War on Drugs: Tools for the Debate*. Bristol, Transform Drug Policy Foundation. Available at: http://www.tdpf.org.uk/Tools_For_The_Debate.pdf

Williams, J. and Wilson, T. (forthcoming) *Work and Lifelong Learning: IFLL Thematic Paper 7*. Leicester, NIACE

Evidence submitted

Alston, E. and Starrs, M. (2008) *Call for Evidence on Lifelong Learning, Crime and Social Exclusion*, South Thames College of Further Education

Betson, S. (2008) *Offender Education in Swedish Prisons – A Report on a Recent Visit*

Brenchley, J. (2008) *Call for Evidence on Lifelong Learning, Crime and Social Exclusion*, Oxford Cambridge and RSA Examinations

Chitty, C. (2008) *What does the evidence tell us about the link between lifelong learning and re-offending?* Ministry of Justice presentation at IFLL seminar.

Duncan, S. (2008) *Inquiry into the Future of Lifelong Learning, Crime and Social Exclusion*, Kent Drug and Alcohol Action Team

Edghill, D. (2008) *Reducing Re-Offending Through Skills and Employment*, Southampton City Council

Freeman, C. (2008) *Lifelong learning, crime and social exclusion*, Touch-type Read and Spell Computer Course

Hooper, B. (2008) *Providing positive activities for young people within library services*, North Yorkshire County Council

Javanaud, P (2008) *Call for Evidence on Lifelong Learning, Crime and Social Inclusion*, Gamesley Community and Adult Community Learning

Lee, M. (2008) '*To reduce crime and disorder and make our communities feel safer*', West Midlands Police

Powell, B. (2008a) *Delivering learndirect in prisons*, Ufi

Powell, B. (2008b) *A best practice guide for learndirect centres in prisons*, Ufi

Savitzky, F. (2008) *Evidence on Lifelong Learning, Crime and Social Exclusion*, London South Bank University

Sweetmore, K. (2008) *Young Offenders Institution Project 2007/2008*, North Yorkshire County Council

Tilley, K. (2008) *An introduction to the Prison Radio Association – learning provider and broadcaster*, The Prison Radio Association

Contributors

Artlandish Ltd

Department for Work and Pensions

Gamesley Community and Adult Community Learning

John Pickin

Kent County Council

London South Bank University

Marketing and Sales Standards Setting Body (MSSSB)

Matrix Knowledge Group

North Yorkshire County Council

OCR (Oxford Cambridge and RSA Examinations)

Paul Ride

Sidney Golding

South Thames College of Further Education

Southampton City Council

The Prison Radio Association

Touch-type Read and Spell Computer Course, Kent

University for Industry (Ufi)

West Midlands Police

Appendix A: Performance measures surrounding offender learning and skills and their possible adverse impacts[85]

Delivery chain partner	Performance measures	Possible perverse incentives
Department for Innovation, Universities and Skills	**Improve the skills of the population** on the way to ensuring a world-class skills base by 2029. Achievement of this Public Service Agreement is measured in terms of the number of adults achieving basic, intermediate and higher level skills qualifications.	Target provision towards those who most likely to achieve qualifications rather than those who are most likely to reduce their chance of re-offending through learning and skills.
Ministry of Justice	**Reduce re-offending through the improved management of offenders**. No target has been set for the rate at which re-offending must be reduced. Prison Service and Probation Service activities will also contribute to this objective.	
Prison Service	**Classroom attendance measures** to maximise the number of offenders attending OLASS funded classes. Classroom attendance rate is defined as actual number of attendees divided by planned number of attendees. A target of 80 per cent is set for each establishment. Purposeful activity targets. All establishments are required to provide a certain level of purposeful activity, calculated as the total number of eligible hours divided by the population. A range of activities qualify as purposeful activity, including all learning and skills.	Encourages the Prison Service to fill class spaces without consideration for who is participating. Does not incentivise enrolling 'hard to reach' groups who are less likely to attend regularly. Does not incentivise prioritising provision for those offenders with the greatest learning and skills needs. Individuals working in prison industries, may, in some cases, learn transferable skills, but may miss out from being assessed for, and accessing, the learning and skills offer within OLASS.
National Probation Service	**Target for referrals to learning and skills.** A different target is set for each probation area. For 2006-07, the target number was 48,000. **Target for getting offenders into work**. A different target is set for each probation area for the number of offenders achieving and sustaining employment for four weeks or more. For 2007-08, the national target was 13,200.	Encourages maximum referrals but there is no need to consider who is being referred or to follow up on the outcomes of referrals. Staff may attach higher priority to getting offenders into work regardless of sustainability, which could mean addressing the learning and skills needs they have over a longer term is less of a priority.

[85] Source: National Audit Office (2008).

Delivery chain partner	Performance measures	Possible perverse incentives
Providers	**Deliver contracted number of teaching hours.**	Does not incentivise the achievement of qualifications and learning progression. Does not incentivise revising the curriculum to deliver more expensive courses, even if these would meet need or increase employability prospects.

Appendix B: The priorities the Learning and Skills Council proposes to attach to different groups of learners[86]

Offender learning curriculum area	Learner target group	Purpose of learning and skills provision	Priority for LSC OLASS funding
Skills for Employment offer	Offenders with sentences less than 12 months to serve.	To provide a short intensive programme and direct offenders to provision on release, acknowledging the limits on provision for those in custody for short periods.	High
Skill for Life offer	Offenders needing basic skills provision, who are ready to learn, who will require at least a year to make progress.	To address needs of those with basic skills needs, working towards national qualifications following further assessment.	High
First full Level 2 offer	Offenders with at least two full years prior to release and preparing for resettlement.	To provide further assessments of need and learning support requirements, and provide a full programme of learning and skills to NVQ Level 2.	High
Young people	Young people in custody.	To provide a full range of learning and skills.	High
Learning for living and work: communication and personal skills	Offenders with learning difficulties and/or disabilities.	To provide additional support to enable engagement in learning.	Medium

---

[86] Source: National Audit Office (2008).